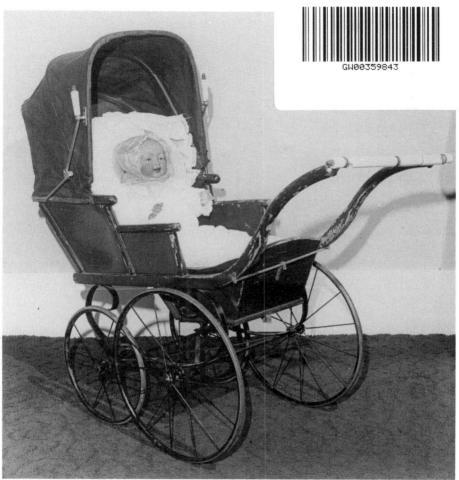

A German bisque 'character' baby doll by Kley and Hahn of Germany, made in 1913, in a doll's pram of about 1900, in the Burrows Toy Museum, Bath.

OLD TOYS

Pauline Flick

Shire Publications Ltd

CONTENTS

Set in 9 point Times Roman and printed in Great Britain by C. I. Thomas & Sons (Haverfordwest) Ltd, Press Buildings, Merlins Bridge, Haverfordwest, Dyfed.

British Library Cataloguing in Publication data available.

ACKNOWLEDGEMENTS
   Photographs on the following pages are acknowledged to: Her Majesty the Queen, 11 (upper); Arundel Toy and Military Museum, 27 (upper); Bethnal Green Museum of Childhood (Crown copyright), 14 (lower); Bowes Museum, 13 (lower); British Museum, 3; Buckley's Museum of Shops, 25 (lower); Burrows Toy Museum, 1, 16 (upper), 22 (lower); Castle Museum, Norwich, 9; Courtauld Institute of Art, 6; Germanisches Nationalmuseum, 7 (upper); National Maritime Museum, 10; Public Records Office, 21 (lower); Science Museum, 12 (upper), 14 (upper); Sotheby's, cover, 2, 21 (upper), 24 (lower), 26 (left); Victoria and Albert Museum, 5, 7 (lower), 8, 12 (lower), 13 (upper), 15 (lower); Worthing Museum, 15 (upper). All other illustrations are from the author's collection.

COVER: *A selection of dolls, teddy bears and other toys from a variety of manufacturers and periods (by courtesy of Sotheby's).*

BELOW: *A dog orchestra; a printed paper automaton with clockwork movement, made in France around 1890.*

An Egyptian toy tiger, made of wood and with a string-operated movable jaw, dating from about 1000 BC and now in the British Museum.

EARLY HISTORY

Since all young creatures instinctively try to copy adult behaviour, the great majority of toys have always reflected the child's attempts to imitate grown-ups. The obvious example, found all over the world, is the little girl with her doll, but models of farm animals, furniture, soldiers, cars and now spacecraft are all part of the same unchanging pattern. Nobody knows when children first made mud pies, sailed pieces of bark or realised that acorn cups made perfect miniature drinking vessels, but such improvisations must be nearly as old as civilisation itself. As for the purpose-made toy — the artefact created specifically as a child's plaything — its early history is no less obscure, and almost nothing is known of any toys before those of the ancient Egyptians.

TOYS IN ANCIENT TIMES

As early as 2000 BC wooden ship models and tableaux representing brewing, baking and other domestic occupations were being made in Egypt. However, these delightful objects, so toy-like in our eyes, were not playthings but funerary offerings, placed in tombs to help the dead on their journey to the next world. Undisturbed for centuries, they have survived intact in a way no mere toy could be expected to have done, and some beautiful examples are on display in the British Museum. Although it is tempting to argue that craftsmen capable of making such lively miniatures probably produced other small things for children's amusement, the first true toys to have been preserved date from about a thousand years later. The British Museum's collection includes a wooden tiger with string-operated snapping jaws, a leg-less cow and some balls made of papyrus. They are not very impressive, but it is fortunate that they have survived at all.

Far more is known about the toys of ancient Greek and Roman children. Contemporary literature, decorated vases and archaeological excavations combine to show that amongst other things they had clay rattles, jointed clay dolls, handcarts, hobby-horses and miniature furniture; in Greece it was the custom for girls to sacrifice their out-grown dolls to the goddess Artemis, and boys their hoops and tops to Hermes. The Romans even had rag dolls: one was found in a child's grave, and this sad little relic, too, can now be seen in the British Museum.

THE MIDDLE AGES

It might be supposed that toys evolved steadily from these promising beginnings, but this was far from being the case. Toymaking flourishes only in the context of a settled way of life, where houses have space for playthings to be kept, and where there is leisure enough for them to be enjoyed. More important still, society must have an indulgent attitude towards its children. Life for affluent Egyptians, Greeks and Romans was sufficiently well ordered for this luxury, but in the dark ages following the collapse of the Roman Empire, and in the middle ages to a lesser degree, existence was too unsettled and precarious for children to be given much special consideration. Almost as soon as a little boy or girl was old enough to play he or she would have been capable of learning to use weapons and tools; in any event, the complete lack of mass production techniques and the difficulties of communication and transport made it hard to obtain even the barest necessities, let alone toys. A few medieval illuminated manuscripts show simple playthings — tops, hobby-horses, puppets and windmills — not very different from those of the Greeks. Anything more elaborate would have been only for the very rich, like the magnificent model soldiers given to young German princelings.

However, the seeds of the German toy industry were sown in the middle ages, and Germany was later to play an outstanding part in the world's toy trade. Wood carving came naturally to country people surrounded by dense forests, and south Germany in particular had a long tradition of making religious figures, especially for Christmas cribs. During the long winters peasants would fill in their time and probably earn a little money by carving simple household utensils and small playthings. At first the trade was purely local; the cost of transporting such intrinsically valueless articles in any quantity would have been prohibitive, but as time went on and communications improved these German toys found their way all over Europe and beyond. Merchants and other travellers, many of them bound for the great fair at Leipzig, gladly bought the various local products and by the early sixteenth century a pattern of toy trading had emerged. Nuremberg was already recognised as an international marketing centre, and soon the neighbouring districts specialising in toys — Oberammergau, the Groden Valley, Berchtesgaden and Sonneberg — were sending goods there to be handled by experienced agents.

It is not known how many of these early German toys reached Britain. Various simple toys were carried round the country by hawkers and pedlars and offered for sale at fairs held in most towns at regular intervals; but these might well have been made in quite small numbers at home, either by the pedlar or by members of his family, much as gypsies still make clothes pegs and paper flowers. Ben Jonson, writing in 1614, mentions hobby-horses, gingerbread figures, miniature animals, dolls, fiddles and drums all being sold at Smithfield's Bartholomew Fair, and it is possible that some of these things were imported: there is no evidence of their production being organised in England on any significant scale.

4

English wooden dolls of the late seventeenth century. Known as 'Lord and Lady Clapham', they retain their original clothes, accessories and chairs.

THE EIGHTEENTH CENTURY

The history of toys changed course dramatically in the eighteenth century, with the dawning of a new era for English children. Until this time English parents had regarded their children as miniature grown-ups, dressing them in stiff adult clothing and expecting them to occupy themselves exclusively with learning and hard work in preparation for later life; the idea of play for its own sake was foreign to a society still deeply influenced by puritan values. Now, however, far more liberal views were gaining ground, reflecting the opinions of enlightened educationalists like John Locke and Isaac Watts; parents began to realise that their children had a right to enjoy themselves, and that sometimes lessons could be learned more quickly if they were combined with an element of entertainment. And with this realisation came — at least from the upper classes — an unprecedented demand for toys.

The change was a gradual one, with many of the new toys turning out to be disappointingly 'improving', but by about 1750 the attitude to childhood was softening in a remarkable way. A number of playthings of this period have survived, such as heavy wooden dolls with dark glass eyes, and we know even more about them from contemporary pictures and diaries. Mrs Delany, Horace Walpole and Parson Woodforde all refer to toys — miniature tea sets, dolls, shops and, in Woodforde's case, a paper caravan bought in Norwich for one shilling and sixpence. Reynolds, Zoffany, Morland

'Sportive Innocence', an engraving of about 1785 by F. Bartolozzi after William Hamilton, RA.

and William Hamilton were among the artists of this time who painted English children enjoying themselves with pet animals and playing with dolls, ships, pull-along horses and other toys far more spectacular than any that had gone before.

This new consideration for children would in itself have been enough to stimulate the toy trade, but equally important were the completely new industrial techniques that swept Europe at about the same time. Hitherto virtually all toys had been made of wood or earthenware, and by hand; but now revolutionary methods of production were applied to new materials. Paper was used increasingly, for board games and beautifully engraved cut-out models, and mass-produced metal toys came on to the market for the first time.

Some of the earliest of these metal figures were made by the Hilpert family of Nuremberg towards the end of the eighteenth century. As well as soldiers the Hilperts produced charming rococo gardens with hedges and fountains, and sets of animals accurately based on detailed drawings, complete with the creatures' Latin names engraved on the stands, giving the toys an extra educational value.

Even comparatively poor families could afford paper toys, since they could be bought as flat engraved sheets to be cut out and made up at home. There were paper soldiers, paper rooms with cut-out figures to stick on to them and paper dolls with an assortment of detachable clothes. This simple toy, endlessly updated with changing fashions in dress, has never lost its appeal. It reached a peak of popularity in the 1930s when large Shirley Temple paper dolls appeared, accompanied by film-star outfits. Its origins, however, go back at least to the late eighteenth century, and it seems to have been an English invention: these little paper figures were always known as 'English dolls', even in Germany.

Paper peepshows, pulling out concertina-fashion, consisted of some dramatic view cut out in several planes arranged one behind another in proper perspective. Scenes of fireworks and illuminations or vistas with baroque fountains were popular early subjects; later on toy peepshows were sold as souvenirs at the opening of the Thames Tunnel and at the Great Exhibition of 1851.

DOLLS' HOUSES

Besides toys from shops, there were sturdy models made by carpenters em-

6

Some examples of the moulded metal animals made in Nuremberg by the Hilpert family, about 1780.

ployed on English country estates; dolls' houses, miniature furniture and scaled-down replicas of carriages and farm wagons from the eighteenth century have all been preserved. The dolls' houses, or 'baby-houses' as they were then called, were often very impressive, and some can still be seen. Model houses had first been made in Germany and the Netherlands, not as children's toys but as cabinets for the display of valuable miniature objects;

English baby-houses, however, seem always to have been much more toy-like than these early continental examples. One of the oldest to have survived was certainly intended for a child, being a gift from Queen Anne to her god-daughter Ann Sharp about 1700: this fully fur-nished house still has its original dolls, labelled with their names — 'Fanny Long, ye Chambermaid', 'Roger ye But-ler', 'Mrs Hannah ye Housekeeper' and

Books intended for the instruction of children, in decorative wooden cases; made in England in the early nineteenth century.

several others of higher social standing.

Another remarkable dolls' house is at Nostell Priory, near Wakefield in West Yorkshire, built by the estate carpenter about 1740. The architect James Paine was then working on Nostell Priory itself, and the baby-house follows broadly the same style, with Ionic columns and pediment. This is such a magnificent toy that it can never have been played with except under the strictest supervision — indeed it was evidently intended primarily to amuse the ladies of the family — and its marble chimney pieces, exquisite fenders, wall-papers, bed-hangings and even the tinder box are still like new after more than two centuries. Several other wonderful baby houses of this period are on view in museums and houses open to the public, notably the elaborate example at Up-park, in West Sussex, the Tate Baby-house in the Bethnal Green Museum, and Mrs Graham Greene's unique collection at The Rotunda, in Oxford.

EDUCATIONAL TOYS

In some ways these early dolls' houses could be classed as 'teaching' toys, since they showed girls the uses of an array of domestic utensils and inspired them to stitch away at needlework carpets and tiny chintz curtains. Other more blatantly improving toys of the period included pictorial alphabet cards, miniature book-cases filled with little volumes on history and scripture, and dissected map puzzles (forerunners of the modern jigsaw), from which a child was expected to absorb geography painlessly. These puzzles, together with the growing number of juvenile books and board games, were mostly produced by London printers and mapmakers trading in the district round St Paul's Cathedral; map puzzles were in existence by the early 1760s, and the poet William Cowper describes a four-year-old boy knowing 'the situation of every kingdom, country, city, river and remark-able mountain in the world' as a result of these ingenious teaching aids. History, too, could be learned from dissected puzzles, and so could moral precepts. One published in 1789 was labelled 'for the instruction of Youth ... to impress upon their minds a love to virtue and a hatred to vice' and had for its picture a tree with the fruits of evil — stealing, lying and gaming — hanging from bare branches, while the fruits of goodness — bravery, sobriety and so forth — flourish on other branches of great luxuriance. Made of mahogany and packed in stout mahogany boxes, these puzzles were not cheap; they cost between seven and twelve shillings, more than many fathers earned in a week, and like many other playthings were still only for the rich.

English picture alphabet cards and their wooden box, made in England about 1830.

8

The lid of a dissected 'French and English Puzzle' of about 1810.

THE NINETEENTH CENTURY

Growing industrialisation in the early nineteenth century brought new toys to the English market in a steady stream, huge quantities being imported from Germany. Illustrated catalogues were already being issued by Nuremberg wholesalers before 1800, and these documents are invaluable in dating toys. Over twelve hundred items are listed in one of the first known catalogues, Bestelmeir's, including tin soldiers, balancing and mechanical figures, houses and gardens to arrange on a table, tiny carriages and air balloons and page after page of other toys. Nelson's little daughter Horatia was painted holding a doll, and a boat, a carriage and a few of her other playthings are displayed at the National Maritime Museum, Greenwich. Early in the century small toys were in demand for decorating Christmas trees: John Watkins, in his *Memoirs of Queen Charlotte* published in 1819, describes a Christmas party at Windsor with 'an immense tub

with a yew-tree placed in it, from the branches of which hung bunches of sweet-meats . . . fruits and toys, most tastefully arranged, and the whole illuminated by small wax candles . . . each child obtained a portion of the sweets which it bore, together with a toy.'

Several of Queen Victoria's childhood possessions are exhibited at Kensington Palace and the Museum of London, including the small wooden dolls she and her governess dressed with such care, a musical box with dancing figures and an austere two-roomed dolls' house. A Biberach catalogue of about 1836 in the Bethnal Green Museum shows that the range of toys then offered was wider than ever; mounted stags' heads for dolls' house halls were just one instance of the German toymakers' originality. The famous wooden soldiers that so delighted the Bronte children, inspiring their amazing fantasies about the imaginary land of Angria, also belong to this period.

An early nineteenth-century portrait of Lord Nelson's daughter Horatia, aged five, holding a doll.

Besides these invaluable trade catalogues, other useful sources of information are the Patent Office Registers and, from 1842 onwards, the Design Registers in the Public Record Office at Kew. The Patent Office documents reveal, for example, that the kaleidoscope, with its ever changing patterns of coloured glass, was patented by Sir David Brewster as early as 1817. Other optical toys were soon to follow, based on the phenomenon of the persistence of vision: the idea behind them was very simple, often demonstrated by a child waving a sparkler round in an apparently un-broken circle of light on Guy Fawkes Night. Introduced in 1826, the thaumatrope was the first of these persistence of vision toys, consisting of a cardboard disc with a related drawing on either side, a bird and a cage, perhaps, or a horse and jockey. The disc was rotated by means of threads attached to opposite points on the circumference, and the eye saw both images together, hence the bird appeared to be in the cage, and the rider on the horse. The first *moving* picture illusion was produced by the phenakistoscope (also called the stroboscope and fantascope), which worked by presenting the eye with a rapid succession of figures in slightly different positions. The figures were drawn on a cardboard disc, which had to be rotated very fast in front of a mirror; the reflected pictures were viewed through slots cut round the edge of the disc and appeared to be moving.

The zoetrope, introduced about 1860, and the slightly later praxinoscope were improvements based on the same idea as the phenakistoscope, and the way these developments led eventually to the true moving picture film is clearly demonstrated by a series of exhibits in the Science Museum, London.

Many other toys are listed in the Patent Office Registers of the nineteenth century. In 1823 came what sounds like the invention of roller skates: 'a machine to be attached to boots, shoes or other covering for the feet, for the purpose of travelling or pleasure'. A discovery that must have been warmly welcomed concerned 'Improvements to Pharoah's serpent', the great improvement being that this popular indoor firework no longer smelled so strongly of sulpho-cyanide of mercury. India rubber and gutta-percha were new materials featured in toy patents of the 1850s, and there are detailed specifications of complicated mechanisms for making wooden horses gallop and dolls walk. The best known walking doll was probably the Autoperipatetikos, first appearing in the United States in 1862, and patented in England in the same year. These dolls must have been fitted with exceptionally strong clockwork, for a great many of them, with their high-stepping metal feet, are still in perfect working order and can be seen in several

RIGHT: *Queen Victoria's dolls' house. A similar house is displayed in the royal nurseries at Osborne House on the Isle of Wight, following renovation by English Heritage in 1988.*

BELOW: *A page from a German toymaker's catalogue of about 1840, showing a Noah's ark complete with animals and human crew.*

The two sides of a thaumatrope disc from the mid 1820s. It is a simple optical toy based on the persistence of vision.

museum collections.

Innumerable playthings have survived from the middle years of the nineteenth century. Labour was still cheap enough for many of them to be finished by hand, and the painted Noah's arks, the lovely Montanari wax dolls and the japanned tinplate trains are minor works of art. The toys belonging to Queen Victoria's children give an idea of the high quality of nursery items then being made: beautifully dressed dolls (Tunbridge Wells Museum and Bethnal Green Museum), miniature wheelbarrows and gardening tools, a set of perfect scaled-down dining chairs and an exquisite model of a grocer's shop are a few of the royal playthings now on public display. Many other valuable toys were evidently carefully looked after, and from the abundance still to be found today it might be supposed that there were no casualties. But the breakage rate for china dolls must have been high, and wax dolls were even more vulnerable. Although Noah's arks, because of their biblical connection, were often kept as Sunday toys and thus escaped some of the rough and tumble of nursery life, their animal inmates were notoriously

An English toy stage coach of around 1830, now in the Bethnal Green Museum.

ABOVE: *A marquetry Noah's ark made in Germany in the nineteenth century.*
BELOW: *A dolls' house room of around 1830, now in the Bowes Museum, Barnard Castle.*

13

brittle and would soon suffer broken legs, ears or tails. Added to these accidental disasters, even Victorian children could be destructive: a horrifying book illustration by A. B. Houghton shows a boy re-enacting the execution of Mary Queen of Scots by beheading his sister's doll with a saw from his model carpentry set.

But if some toys were broken there was no lack of replacements. In London toy emporiums like the Lowther Arcade, the Soho Bazaar and Cremer's of Regent Street overflowed with every sort of delight. One curmudgeon complained about shopkeepers who blocked the passageways of the Lowther Arcade (north of the Strand, near Charing Cross) with drums, children's tea things, Birmingham and Wedgwood trumperies, rocking horses and lambswool poodles. Besides these there were model theatres (penny plain, and tuppence coloured), magic lanterns, dolls of all kinds, clockwork trains, musical automata, doll's houses complete with every imaginable piece of furniture, three-wheeled prams, balancing figures, model shops, building bricks and castellated forts — the vast plenty of the mid nineteenth-century toyshop defies being catalogued: no mere stock-list can com-

14

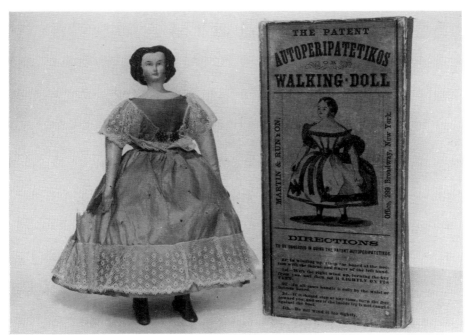

ABOVE: *The American 'Autoperipatetikos' clockwork mechanical doll, with its original box.*

BELOW: *A German clockwork tin train of about 1840, together with its original box.*

15

RIGHT: *A dolls' house of 1880. Made of wood, it is covered with varnished paper with a brick design.*

BELOW: *A German baby doll of about 1850 in a toy cradle made a century before.*

An English wax doll of the mid nineteenth century.

17

pete with Dickens' picture in *The Cricket on the Hearth* of Tackleton the toy merchant with his 'hideous, hairy, red-eyed Jacks-in-Boxes . . . brown-paper farmers who drove pigs to market . . . movable old ladies who darned stockings or carved pies . . . and demoniacal Tumblers who wouldn't lie down, and were perpetually flying forward, to stare infants out of countenance'. A few pages later we find Caleb Plummer and his blind daughter in their workroom surrounded by 'houses for Dolls of all stations in life . . . scores of melancholy little carts which performed most doleful music . . . There were little tumblers in red breeches, incessantly swarming up high obstacles of red-tape, and coming down, head first, on the other side . . . There were beasts of all sorts, horses in particular, of every breed, from the spotted barrel on four pegs, with a small tippet for a mane, to the thoroughbred rocker on his highest mettle.' Descrip-

tions like this are interesting for the light they throw on the ordinary, everyday plaything of the new middle class; usually it is the more expensive toys which survive in museums, as these were treated more carefully. But *The Cricket on the Hearth* has immortalised the expendable companions of a generation of children 'who had played with them, and found them out, and broken them, and gone to sleep'. The original illustrations by John Leech are equally valuable, for the drawings of Caleb's workroom and all the toys are marvellously detailed.

Although mid Victorian toyshops were still stocked largely with goods imported from Germany, English makers were famous for sturdy wooden toys, wax dolls, humming tops, board games and miniature tea and dinner services. These pottery toys, mostly from Staffordshire, were turned out by the thousand and are charming things to collect. Even in the

A collection of mid nineteenth-century dolls' house furniture in imitation rosewood, made in Germany. The two larger dolls date from the late nineteenth century.

A miniature screen of the late nineteenth century, with scenes from fairy tales, suitable for a dolls' house, and advertising Dr Lovelace's Soap.

eighteenth century miniature pieces had been made for baby-houses — there is a set of delicate pierced Leeds ware in Ann Sharp's house — but as soon as transfer printing on earthenware became a practical proposition mugs and plates cheap enough for children to use had been produced. At first the decorations tended to be improving or educational, with many moral verses and biblical scenes, but soon the subjects grew more light-hearted, often combining the letters of the alphabet with a cheerful nursery illustration. Earthenware tea and dinner services for dolls were made from about 1820 and huge numbers are still to be found, complete with tureens, sauce boats, ladles and dozens of assorted plates; they were decorated in a variety of patterns, some with scaled-down versions of familiar blue and white designs and later examples with fairy-story characters or nursery scenes. Other pottery toys included carpet bowls and decorated eggs (from Sunderland) and salt-glazed money boxes; Wedgwood has revived the idea of a pottery money box and now makes one with Peter Rabbit decorations.

But there were countless children who suffered rather than benefited from the industrial revolution; many of them, often only eight years old, were employed in the Potteries as well as in mills and mines, and an official report of 1842 mentions William Cotton, a boy of nine from Longton, who worked for seventy hours a week and earned two shillings for making nearly three thousand earthenware figures. Conditions gradually improved, thanks to Lord Shaftesbury and other social reformers, but for many children the reforms came too late. Even Flora Thompson, who wrote so movingly of her comparatively happy childhood in *Lark Rise to Candleford*, hardly mentions toys, and as a working-class child living deep in the country in the 1880s she probably saw very few. For her, the May Day doll, kept in the school needlework box and brought out once a year for the traditional village procession, was still a thing of wonder.

There were, however, some interesting little toys of this period that cost nothing: these were the free gifts offered by various firms, usually in exchange for coupons collected from their products.

The Harris Museum at Preston has three cheap wax dolls given in return for tea coupons in the 1880s, but it was the soap manufacturers who seem to have been by far the most active in this sales promotion field, offering an assortment of delightful paper toys (Sunlight Soap, 1896) and a charming *art nouveau* screen for a dolls' house (Lovelace's Soap, about 1895). Pear's Soap gave away colour reproductions of well known pictures, suitable for framing, with their shilling Christmas annuals, bringing *Bubbles, Cherry Ripe* and other childhood favourites to many walls that would otherwise have remained bare.

Other toys were distributed at Christmas to sick and needy children, bought with the proceeds of bazaars and fancy fairs that were such a feature of late nineteenth-century charity. *Truth* magazine asked its readers to provide toys (with a prize for the best home-made entry) for a huge toy show, after which the thousands of toys submitted were taken to the young patients in London's hospitals and workhouses. Within a few years this annual event had become so popular that the organisers had to stage it in the Albert Hall.

CHANGES IN FASHION AND TECHNIQUE

Rich children with indulgent parents had nurseries full of toys. Towards the end of the nineteenth century there were even more metal goods — tinplate ships and trains, filigree dolls' house furniture and clockwork figures — and novelties such as heavy stone building blocks and superb French dolls. Jumeau and Bru were the most famous Parisian doll-making firms, and their dolls can be recognised by their expressive faces and, in the case of the Jumeaus, their huge owl-like eyes. Often trunkloads of clothes and accessories came with them, so they could be dressed in the latest fashion. Other expensive dolls of this period could walk, talk or swim, and there were others with two or three faces so that they could be made to sleep, smile or cry at the turn of a knob on top of the head. One three-faced doll that must have alarmed many a sensitive child combined the characters of Red Riding Hood, the Grandmother and the Wolf.

Not all parents approved of such elaborate playthings, and then as now there was much heart-searching among intellectuals as to what constituted a good and healthy toy. Ellen Terry would only let her children have things made of wood, and if a friend gave them anything she considered unsuitable it was immediately taken away and burned. A clockwork mouse suffered this fate, condemned as 'realistic and common'. The darling of such aesthetic families was Walter Crane: besides designing children's books revolutionary in their simplicity, he produced wallpapers with fairy-

An advertisement of 1896 by Sunlight Soap showing the various paper toys available to purchasers of their products.

story characters woven into sinuous patterns of pale blues, greens and yellows, which were eagerly bought by mothers with pre-Raphaelite leanings.

Advances in printing techniques played a large part in the development of toys in the second half of the nineteenth century. With the increasing use of chromolithography there were far more books with coloured illustrations, and it is sometimes difficult to draw the line between toys and nursery books: there were books about animals, for example, containing a bellows mechanism so that animal noises were emitted when appropriate strings were pulled; bright pop-up scenes sprang into life at the turn of a page, and other books for the very young were shaped like dolls and animals. Ernest Nister and Raphael Tuck are names to look for on printed goods of the 1890s: both of these London firms produced beautiful nursery

RIGHT: *A rare walking and talking doll, made by Bru of France around 1895.*

BELOW: *'Nursery Rhymes' wallpaper, produced by Walter Crane in 1876.*

21

books, and Tucks also made postcards, paper doll sets and embossed cardboard animals with movable limbs (they also added the animals' Latin names, just as the Hilperts had done a century before).

Much of the colour printing was still done in Bavaria, where the best lithographic stone was to be found. Boxed scenes, with moving figures driven by clockwork or falling sand, relied for much of their appeal on their printed pictures; embossed paper scraps were another German speciality exported to England, angelic-looking girls, puppies, kittens and brilliant flowers being the most usual subjects; scrap screens of this period are now much in demand, and nothing evokes more keenly the atmosphere of late Victorian nurseries with their nannies, brass fireguards and fumes from the magic lantern.

RIGHT: *A 'Trick Pony', an American iron money box of the late nineteenth century.*

BELOW: *A kitchen made in Germany around the end of the nineteenth century. The cooking range is heated with a spirit lamp while a working electric light and switch (right, above table) were added at a later date.*

Early box covers (dating from the early twentieth century) of Harbutt's Plasticine.

THE TWENTIETH CENTURY

EDWARDIAN TOYS

Edwardian toymakers were as enterprising as ever, and with the new century British firms began to rival their German competitors. William Harbutt had invented Plasticine in 1897 and, although beginning in a small way, the business soon prospered, once the educational uses of the new material were recognised. One of the pleasures of collecting playthings of this vintage is to find a toy still with its original box, as the lids were often charmingly decorated; one of Harbutt's first outfits was called 'The Child's Delight' and showed two children modelling a large elephant. Similar lids giving an exaggerated idea of the contents were used for boxes of building bricks — usually implying that a towering edifice could be constructed from the smallest box — and nursery games were shown being played by laughing families in immaculate evening dress.

Another firm with a long and successful history is Britains, now best known for toy soldiers, which were first produced in the 1890s. Farmyards, zoos, Boy Scout encampments, cowboys and Indians were gradually added to the range, as well as some dolls' house accessories priced at a penny each: the coal scuttle and high chair can often be picked out in dolls'

houses of about 1910.

New ground was also broken by Dean's Rag Book Company, founded in 1903, when Henry Samuel Dean saw the advantages of indestructible fabric picture books for the very young. Several well known artists provided drawings for the first rag books, including John Hassall, Hilda Cowham and Cecil Aldin, and they are still popular today. Other early Dean's toys were Punch and Judy puppets, jointed cloth dolls, printed cotton sheets for making up into dolls and animals, and furry pets.

The first known Bassett-Lowke catalogue appeared in 1901, and for the next thirty years or more it was every boy's dream to own one of the model steam locomotives manufactured by this firm. At Bassett-Lowke's shop in High Holborn engineering marvels like the model of Stephenson's *Rocket* ('strong brass boiler, patent spirit lamp, double-action slide valve cylinders, whistle and safety valve') and locomotives of the famous Black Prince series could be bought. Besides the engines produced in his Northampton factory, J. J. Bassett-Lowke arranged for various German firms to supply him with models specially adapted for the British market: the well known Bing Table Railways were one

LEFT: *A Dean's Rag Book and a printed cotton 'Dog Toby' (Mr Punch's companion) of the early twentieth century.*

BELOW: *A musical automaton. Made in France in 1910, this fur-covered rabbit chews a piece of lettuce and waves its ears to the sound of music.*

result of this association.

Frank Hornby was another English toymaker whose name became a household word. As well as being celebrated for clockwork and electric trains he was the inventor of Meccano, which he developed after watching a crane near the Liverpool office where he worked. In 1901 he took out a patent for a constructional toy made up of perforated metal parts, but it was some years before he could persuade a manufacturer that Mechanics Made Easy — the original name — was a commercial proposition. The Meccano company also made Dinky cars, designed to complement Hornby model railway layouts. After giving untold pleasure to countless children the old Meccano company and several other well known diecasting firms had to cease trading in the 1960s and 1970s, faced with changing fashions and fierce foreign competition.

The British gollywog is another toy with an uncertain future, but for quite different reasons. This delightful childhood friend first appeared in Florence Upton's book *The Adventures of Two Dutch Dolls and a Golliwogg,* published in 1895. The mischievous black doll was an immediate nursery favourite, and manufacturers, including Dean, were soon making toy versions. 'Golly' was also adopted by Robertsons, the marma-

ABOVE: *Items from a toy dinner service, decorated with Kate Greenaway drawings from 'Mother Goose', made in England about 1900.*

BELOW: *Early twentieth-century German bisque-headed dolls.*

lade makers, as a trademark, and it featured in a host of trade promotions. Now some people think that the gollywog embodies racist feelings and should be banned.

The best-loved Edwardian innovation of all, the teddy bear, was not a British invention. The cub that unwittingly inspired a new industry was American: President Theodore Roosevelt had declined to shoot the little animal while on a hunting trip in 1902, and a political cartoonist made a drawing of the incident. The first toy bear based on the drawing appears to have been made by an American, Morris Michtom, but at about the same time Margaret Steiff, a talented German toymaker, was working on cuddly plush bears. Steiff's American agent was so enthusiastic about them that he immediately ordered three thousand, and since then the teddy bear has remained a universal favourite.

Alongside all the novelties of the early twentieth century, with its new ideas and streamlined production methods, many old favourites were holding their own. Magic lanterns, known in England since the 1660s, still provided nursery entertainment and a wide assortment of slides, ranging from 'The Three Bears' to 'Our Lifeboatmen', could be purchased in 1907. Other well tried playthings were adapted to suit an ever growing market where low prices were of paramount importance. In 1910 a Nuremberg firm was able to offer a collapsible Noah's ark with twenty-four animals at eight shillings and eight pence per *dozen,* wholesale. Cardboard was used for Jolly Jumpers, amusing little jointed figures derived from the Victorian jumping jack and even earlier French *pantin;* rather flimsy shops and dolls' houses tended to replace the sturdy wooden versions of earlier years, although many high-quality toys were still being produced for the luxury market.

LEFT: *A 'Pussy Band' of around 1910. The four cats play their instruments, driven by a clockwork mechanism at the rear of this printed paper automaton.*

RIGHT: *'Sunny Jim'. A rag doll advertising 'Force' wheat flakes.*

ABOVE: *Early twentieth-century toys. From left: a Chad Valley musical cat; a French bulldog; a hurdy-gurdy dog with nodding head; Felix the Cat.*

RIGHT: *Dean's 'Dismal Desmond' dogs with a poster announcing a 'Dismal Desmond' Ball at the Hammersmith Palais de Danse in 1927.*

BESTWAY
LEAFLET 3ᵈ
604

TEDDY BEAR, PRAM BALL &
RED RIDING HOOD DOLL'S SET
(Oddments of 3 and 4-ply)

Wartime knitting patterns for toys, produced in Britain in the 1940s.

THE INTER-WAR YEARS

The industry made an amazing recovery after the First World War, and British firms went from strength to strength. However, German manufacturers still had a monopoly of china dolls, supplying not only new dolls but countless replacement heads to dolls' hospitals. Celluloid was increasingly used, despite being dangerously inflammable, and millions of fragile little dolls and animals were imported from Japan.

All kinds of mascot toys date from this period, the best remembered probably being Sunny Jim. This odd-looking rag doll originated in the United States and first came to Britain in the early 1920s; it was (and still is) given in exchange for coupons from Force cereal packets. Many popular cartoon characters were transformed into three-dimensional toys,

including Felix the Cat, Mickey Mouse and Snow White and the Seven Dwarfs. One of Dean's original creations, Dismal Desmond the Dalmatian, became a national figure, lending his name to many good causes, including a Hospital Ball held at the Hammersmith Palais de Danse. Mabel Lucie Attwell characters were everywhere: as early as 1910 this prolific artist had designed a nursery frieze, and her chubby toddlers were used to decorate tableware, fabrics and biscuit tins as well as appearing as dolls. The *Daily Mirror's* Pip, Squeak and Wilfred (a dog, penguin and rabbit) had a tremendous following in the 1920s and 1930s; these famous pets were even turned into tiny china cake decorations.

WARTIME TOYS

With the outbreak of the Second World War in 1939 the European toy trade came virtually to a standstill. British factories switched to making munitions, and only a few home-produced toys reached the shops. Probably the most appealing, from a collector's point of view, were the small velvety servicemen and women made by Norah Wellings. Children generally had to make do with playthings handed down by older brothers and sisters, which may be why toys of the 1930s are comparatively difficult to find, few having survived this double lifespan. There was a boom in patterns for knitted toys, which mothers could make at home, though even these had to be contrived from odds and ends as wool was soon rationed. After the war ended there was still an acute shortage of most raw materials, and it was not until the late 1940s that the trade began to recover.

POST-WAR DEVELOPMENTS

With this gradual recovery came changes as revolutionary as those which had transformed the world of toys in the mid eighteenth century. There was already a vast market in existence and new plastic materials had a profound effect on the industry, replacing china and celluloid for dolls and ousting metal and wood in the manufacture of many other toys. Intense realism has been a feature of many modern products: Action

The Lesney Coronation Coach of 1953.

Man and Sindy dolls, for example, look almost human and demand endless quantities of authentic 'gear' in the way of clothes and equipment. Miniature vehicles are equally realistic, and dolls' house furniture, mostly from the Far East, now rivals the finest antique pieces in its minute detail.

Some of today's toys will doubtless become the museum pieces of tomorrow, and far-sighted investors may well be laying down examples from the electronic age. The Lesney Coronation Coach of 1953 is already a collector's item, and cars and soldiers of the 1930s are much sought after, fetching high prices at sales.

FURTHER READING

Bull, Peter. *Bear With Me*. Hutchinson, 1969.
Cockrill, Pauline. *Teddy Bears and Soft Toys*. Shire, 1988.
Coleman, D. S., E. A. and E. J. *The Collector's Encyclopedia of Dolls*. Robert Hale.
Daiken, Leslie. *Children's Toys throughout the Ages*. Batsford, 1953.
Early, Alice K. *English Dolls, Effigies and Puppets*. Batsford, 1955.
Eaton, Faith. *Dolls in Colour*. Blandford, 1975.
Earnshaw, Nora. *Collecting Dolls*. Collins, 1987.
Flick, Pauline. *Children's China*. Constable, 1983.
Fraser, Antonia. *A History of Toys*. Weidenfeld and Nicholson, 1966.
Fritzch, K. E., and Bachmann, M. *An Illustrated History of Toys*. Abbey Library, 1966.
Gordon, Lesley. *Peepshow Into Paradise*. Harrap, 1953.
Greene, Vivien. *English Dolls' Houses of the Eighteenth and Nineteenth Centuries*. Batsford, 1955.
Groeber, Karl. *Children's Toys of Bygone Days*. Batsford, 1928.
Harley, Basil. *Optical Toys*. Shire, 1988.
Harley, Basil. *Toy Boats*. Shire, 1987.
Hillier, Mary. *Dolls and Dollmakers*. Weidenfeld and Nicholson, 1968.
Hillier, Mary. *Automata and Mechanical Toys*. Jupiter Books, 1976.
Jacobs, Flora Gill. *A History of Dolls' Houses*. Cassell, 1954.
King, Constance E. *Encyclopedia of Toys*. Robert Hale.
Murray, Patrick. *Toys*. Studio Vista, 1968.
Speaight, George. *The History of the English Toy Theatre*. Studio Vista, 1969.
White, Gwen. *European and American Dolls*. Batsford, 1966.
White, Gwen. *Antique Toys and their Background*. Batsford, 1971.
Mr Gamage's Great Toy Bazaar 1902-1906. Denys Ingram, 1982.

PLACES TO VISIT

This is only a selection of the many museums now displaying collections of dolls and toys. Local tourist information centres can give details of other collections or temporary exhibitions. Intending visitors are advised to find out the times of opening before making a special journey.

GREAT BRITAIN

Abbey House Museum, Abbey Road, Kirkstall, Leeds, West Yorkshire LS5 3GH. Telephone: Leeds (0532) 755821.

American Museum in Britain, Claverton Manor, Bath, Avon BA2 7BD. Telephone: Bath (0225) 60503.

Arreton Manor, Newport, Isle of Wight. Telephone: Newport, Isle of Wight (0983) 528134.

Arundel Toy and Military Museum, Dolls House, 23 High Street, Arundel, West Sussex. Telephone: Arundel (0903) 883101 or 882908.

Bankfield Museum, Boothtown Road, Halifax, West Yorkshire. Telephone: Halifax (0422) 54823.

Bantock House, Bantock Park, Merridale Road, Wolverhampton, West Midlands WV3 9LQ. Telephone: Wolverhampton (0902) 312132.

Barum Toy Museum, 11 Boutport Street, Barnstaple, Devon. Telephone: Barnstaple (0271) 43641.

Bedford Museum, Castle Lane, Bedford MK40 3XD. Telephone: Bedford (0234) 53323.

Bethnal Green Museum of Childhood, Cambridge Heath Road, London E2 9PA. Telephone: 01-980 4315.

Birmingham Museum and Art Gallery, Chamberlain Square, Birmingham, West Midlands B3 3DH. Telephone: 021-235 2834.

Blaise Castle House Museum, Henbury, Bristol, Avon BS10 7QS. Telephone: Bristol (0272) 506789.

Botanic Gardens Museum, Churchtown, Southport, Lancashire PR9 7NB. Telephone: Southport (0704) 33133.

Bowes Museum, Barnard Castle, County Durham DL12 8NP. Telephone: Teesdale (0833) 37139.

Bromsgrove Museum, 26 Birmingham Road, Bromsgrove, Worcestershire B61 0DD. Telephone: Bromsgrove (0527) 77934.

Buckley's Museum of Shops, 90 High Street, Battle, East Sussex TN33 0AQ. Telephone: Battle (042 46) 4269.

Cambridge and County Folk Museum, 2 and 3 Castle Street, Cambridge CB3 0AQ. Telephone: Cambridge (0223) 355159.

Childhood Reflections, 13 New Road, Hebden Bridge, West Yorkshire. Telephone: Halifax (0422) 845555.

Cockthorpe Hall Toy Museum, Cockthorpe, Wells-next-the-Sea, Norfolk. Telephone: Binham (032875) 293.

Coventry Toy Museum, Whitefriars Gate, Much Park Street, Coventry, West Midlands. Telephone: Coventry (0203) 27560.

Crow Nest Park Museum, Heckmondwike Road, Dewsbury, West Yorkshire. Telephone: Dewsbury (0924) 468171.

Cumberland Toy and Model Museum, Bank's Court, Market Place, Cockermouth, Cumbria. Telephone: Cockermouth (0900) 823254.

Cuming Museum, 155/157 Walworth Road, London SE17 1RS. Telephone: 01-703 3324.

Educational Museum, High Street, Haslemere, Surrey. Telephone: Haslemere (0428) 2112.

Elizabethan House Museum, 70 Fore Street, Totnes, Devon. Telephone: Totnes (0803) 863821.

Guildford Museum, Castle Arch, Quarry Street, Guildford, Surrey GU1 3SX. Telephone: Guildford (0483) 503497.

Guildhall Museum, High Street, Rochester, Kent. Telephone: Medway (0634) 48717.

Gunnersbury Park Museum, Gunnersbury Park, London W3 8LQ. Telephone: 01-992 1612.

Harris Museum and Art Gallery, Market Square, Preston, Lancashire PR1 2PP. Telephone: Preston (0772) 58248.

Haworth Museum of Childhood, West Lane, Haworth, West Yorkshire BD22 8EE. Telephone: Haworth (0535) 43825.

Helston Folk Museum, Old Butter Market, Market Place, Helston, Cornwall.

Hereford and Worcester County Museum, Hartlebury Castle, Hartlebury, Kidderminster, Worcestershire DY11 7XZ. Telephone: Hartlebury (0299) 250416.

Hereford City Museum and Art Gallery, Broad Street, Hereford HR4 9AU. Telephone: Hereford (0432) 268121.

The Hollytrees, High Street, Colchester, Essex CO1 1UG. Telephone: Colchester (0206) 712493.

Hove Museum of Art, 19 New Church Road, Hove, East Sussex BN3 4AB. Telephone: Brighton (0273) 779410.

Judges' Lodgings, Church Street, Lancaster, Lancashire. Telephone: Lancaster (0524) 32808.

Judy Sparrow's Bear Museum, 38 Dragon Street, Petersfield, Hampshire. Telephone: Petersfield (0730) 65108 or 66962.

Lilian Middleton Antique Doll Collection, Tudor House, Sheep Street, Stow-on-the-Wold, Gloucestershire GL54 1AA. Telephone: Stow-on-the-Wold (0451) 30381.

Lilliput Museum of Antique Dolls and Toys, High Street, Brading, Isle of Wight PO36 0DJ. Telephone: Isle of Wight (0983) 407231.

Little Museum of Childhood, Stansted, Essex. Telephone: Bishops Stortford (0279) 812232. Open by appointment only.

Little Treasures Doll Museum, Ravenhall, Duncan Street, Laugharne, Carmarthen, Dyfed. Telephone: Laugharne (099 421) 554.

Llandudno Doll Museum and Model Railway Exhibition, Masonic Street, Llandudno, Gwynedd. Telephone: Llandudno (0492) 76312.

Luton Museum and Art Gallery, Wardown Park, Luton, Bedfordshire LU2 7HA. Telephone: Luton (0582) 36941.

Michelham Priory, Upper Dicker, Hailsham, East Sussex BN27 3QS. Telephone: Hailsham (0323) 844224.

Museum of Childhood, 1 Castle Street, Beaumaris, Anglesey, Gwynedd LL58 8AP. Telephone: Beaumaris (0248) 810448.

Museum of Childhood, 42 High Street, Edinburgh EH1 1TG. Telephone: 031-225 2424.

Museum of Childhood, Sudbury Hall, Sudbury, Derby DE6 5HT. Telephone: Sudbury (028 378) 305.

Museum of Costume, Alfred Street, Bath, Avon BA1 2QH. Telephone: Bath (0225) 61111.

Museum of London, London Wall, London EC2Y 5HN. Telephone: 01-600 3699.

Museum of Social History, 27 King Street, King's Lynn, Norfolk PE30 1HA. Telephone: King's Lynn (0533) 775004.

Newarke Houses Museum, The Newarke, Leicester LE2 7BY. Telephone: Leicester (0533) 554100.

Nostell Priory, Wakefield, West Yorkshire. Telephone: Wakefield (0924) 863892. Eighteenth-century baby-house.

Penrhyn Castle, Bangor, Gwynedd LL57 4HN. Telephone: Bangor (0248) 353084.

Penshurst Place, Penshurst, Tonbridge, Kent. Telephone: Penshurst (0892) 870307.

Pollock's Toy Museum, 1 Scala Street, London W1P 1LT. Telephone: 01-636 3452.

Precinct Toy Collection, 38 Harnet Street, Sandwich, Kent. Telephone: Thanet (0843) 692150.

Private Museum of Prams, Wild Rock, The Common, Dilhorne, Stoke-on-Trent, Staffordshire. Telephone: Stoke-on-Trent (0782) 396301. By appointment only.

The Priest House, West Hoathly, East Grinstead, West Sussex. Telephone: East Grinstead (0342) 810479.

Red House Museum, Quay Road, Christchurch, Dorset BH23 1BU. Telephone: Christchurch (0202) 482860.

Ribchester Dolls House and Model Museum, Church Street, Ribchester, Lancashire PR3 3YE. Telephone: Ribchester (025484) 520.

Rottingdean Grange (including National Toy Museum), Rottingdean, Brighton, East Sussex BN2 7HA. Telephone: Brighton (0273) 31004.

The Rotunda Museum of Antique Dolls' Houses, Grove House, 44 Iffley Turn, Oxford. Summer Sunday afternoons only, or parties of twelve or more by written appointment; no children under sixteen.

Royal Pump Room Museum, Royal Parade, Harrogate, North Yorkshire. Telephone: Harrogate (0423) 503340.

Rye (Ypres Tower) Museum, 4 Church Square, Rye, East Sussex TN31 7HE. Telephone: Rye (0797) 223254.

Saffron Walden Museum, Museum Street, Saffron Walden, Essex CB10 1JL. Telephone: Saffron Walden (0799) 22494.

Shaftesbury Local History Museum, Gold Hill, Shaftesbury, Dorset. Telephone: Shaftesbury (0747) 2157 or 3426.

Snowshill Manor, near Broadway, Worcestershire WR12 7JU. Telephone: Broadway (0386) 852410.

Staffordshire County Museum, Shugborough, Stafford ST17 0XB. Telephone: Little Haywood (0889) 881388.

Strangers' Hall Museum, Charing Cross, Norwich, Norfolk NR2 4AL. Telephone: Norwich (0603) 611277 extension 275.

The Toy Museum, 42 Bridge Street Row, Chester, Cheshire. Telephone: Chester (0244) 316251.
The Toy Museum, Dedham Arts and Crafts Centre, High Street, Dedham, Colchester, Essex.
Telephone: Colchester (0206) 322666.
Tudor House Museum, St Michael's Square, Southampton, Hampshire. Telephone: Southampton
(0703) 224216.
Tunbridge Wells Municipal Museum, Civic Centre, Mount Pleasant, Tunbridge Wells, Kent TN1
1RS. Telephone: Tunbridge Wells (0892) 26121 extension 171.
Wallington Hall, Wallington, Cambo, Morpeth, Northumberland NE61 4AR. Telephone: Scots
Gap (067 074) 283.
Welsh Folk Museum, St Fagans, Cardiff, South Glamorgan CF5 6XB. Telephone: Cardiff (0222)
569441.
Windsor Castle, Windsor, Berkshire. Telephone: Windsor (075 35) 68286.
Woodspring Museum, Burlington Street, Weston-super-Mare, Avon BS23 1PR. Telephone:
Weston-super-Mare (0934) 21028.
Worthing Museum and Art Gallery, Chapel Road, Worthing, West Sussex BN11 1HD. Telephone:
Worthing (0903) 39999.
York Castle Museum, Tower Street, York, North Yorkshire YO1 1RY. Telephone: York (0904)
653611.

EUROPE

Deutches Spielzeugmuseum (German Toy Museum), Beethovenstrasse 10, 65 Sonneberg, East
Germany.
Frans Hals Museum, Groot Heiligland 62, 2011 RD Haarlem, Noord Holland, Holland.
Gemeente-Museum, The Hague, Holland.
Germanisches Nationalmuseum, Kornmarkt 1, 8500 Nurnberg (Nuremberg), Bavaria, West
Germany.
Hessisches Puppenmuseum, Hanau, Hessen, West Germany.
Musée des Arts Decoratifs, Pavillon de Marsan, 107-9 Rue de Rivoli, 75001 Paris, France.
Musée du Jouet, Rue de l'Association 24, Brussels, Belgium.
Musée du Jouet, 2 Enclo de l'Abbaye, 78300 Poissy, France.
Musée National, 17 Avenue Princesse Grace, Monte Carlo 98000, Monaco.
Das Puppenmuseum, Legge, 4542 Tecklenberg, Nordrhein-Westfalen, West Germany.
Rijksmuseum, Stadhouderskade 42, 1071 XZ, Amsterdam, Noord Holland, Holland.
Spielzeugmuseum der Stadt Nurnberg, Karlstrasse 13, 8500 Nurnberg (Nuremberg), Bavaria, West
Germany.
Stadt Museum, Krummebergstrasse 30, 7770 Uberlingen am Bodensee, Baden-Wurttemberg,
West Germany.

NORTH AMERICA

Black Creek Pioneer Village, 1000 Murray Ross Parkway, Toronto, Ontario, Canada. The Percy
Band Toy Collection.
Essex Institute, 132 Essex Street, Salem, Massachusetts 01970, USA.
Margaret Woodbury Strong Museum, Manhatten Square, Rochester, New York 14607, USA.
Mary Merritt Doll Museum, Route 422, Douglassville, Pennsylvania 19518, USA.
Milwaukee Public Museum, 800 West Wells Street, Milwaukee, Wisconsin 53233, USA.
Miniature Museum, Kansas City, Missouri, USA.
Museum of the City of New York, Fifth Avenue at 103rd Street, New York City, New York 10029,
USA.
Newport Historical Society, 82 Touro Street, Newport, Rhode Island 02840, USA.
Washington Dolls' House and Toy Museum, 5236 44th Street NW, Washington, DC 20015, USA.
Wenham Historical Association and Museum Inc, 132 Main Street, Wenham, Massachusetts 01984,
USA.

AUSTRALIA AND NEW ZEALAND

International Gallery of Dolls, 25 Torrens Street, Victor Harbor, South Australia.
Teddy Museum, 118 Edward Street, Brisbane, Queensland 40000, Australia.
Wanganui Regional Museum, Maria Place, Wanganui, Wellington Province, New Zealand.
Antique doll collection.